COVERED GROUND

COVERED GROUND

Tony Spivey

Iriswhite Publishing
New York

Covered Ground

Copyright ©2002 by Tony Spivey.
All rights reserved.

No part of this book may be reproduced or transmitted in any form or by any means, graphic, electronic, or mechanical, including photocopying, recording, taping, or by any information storage retrieval system, without permission in writing from the author.

Iriswhite Publishing
New York

For information, visit
www.iriswhite.com

ISBN: 0-971-10722-X
Library of Congress Control Number: 2002114879
FIRST EDITION

Printed in the United States of America

This book is dedicated in memory of

Ronnie Lee Crooms
February 1958 - July 1974

My friend.

TABLE OF CONTENTS

Dedication v

Table of Contents vii

Acknowledgments xiii

Looking Back

A Poet Should Not Die Unwritten 4
Forgotten 5
Once 6
Ceramic Clown 7
The Vessel Of Innocence 8
Too Well 11
Old Jill, Dad And Me 12
The Violets Of Our Youth 16
I Don't Know 18
Oh, How I Loved You 20
All I Ever Wanted To Do 22
When We Loved Each Other 24
A Cry Of Understanding 26
How Could It Be? 27
Dance Of The Hummingbirds In June 28
Mr. Adelson Speaks To My Love In The Park 30
Driftwood And Sea Foam 32
Silence In The Wood 32
That Day 33
Dead Stars 34

– Table of Contents –

Here And Now

Covered Ground	36
Tamed	37
This Morning, I Just Watched You Sleep	38
Love Verse	40
Until Time Bows Me Old	40
Your Hands	41
The Moaning Well	42
I'm Leaving	44
On Highway 43	46
I Love You	47
Passing Time At The China Doll	48
On A Gray, Dusty Wall	50
The Silence Of Alone	51
As If	52
In The Rain	54
Just For You	54
I Ache	55
3 A.M. At The Veterans Hospital	56
The Peep Hole	59
First Kiss	60
Under The Glow Of The Moon	61
Quantum Kisses In The Ethereal Garden	62
Tangled Heart Strings	67
Secret Love	68
Your Embrace	68
Black Rain	69
When I Sit Silently Beside You	70
Windless Chimes	71
Toothpaste And Underwear	72
Shadow Dancing	74
Touch My Hand That I May See	74

– Table of Contents –

Quietly Wicked 75
I Know Her In Words 76
Tonight 77
Holding On 78
Eight Thousand Days 80
Brush Strokes 80
First Light Of Day 81
To Steal From The Devil 82
Without Regret 83
I Am The Sea 84
Blame Me 84
She Is 85
Secrets Scripted 86
Blue Pennies Down 87
My Love Is A Simple Love 88
This Love Is Not Misplaced 89
Gently 90
The Taste Of Her Soul 91
Captured 92
Black Sleep 94
Beyond The Fall 95
The Procession 96
Rain On The Window 97
Wild Horses 98
Sometimes 100
Ashes 101
Just For Me 102
Where Ever You Are 104
The Man In The Moon 106
Memories In The Dark 107
Say Not The Words 108

– Table of Contents –

Dreams

The Laugh Of True Lovers 110
Travels Of The Same Time 111
Across The Distance 112
To Rest Upon A Calmer Shore 113
Where A Princess Meets The Sea 114
Dreaming Of You 115
Twilight 116
Forbidden Dreams 116
Curtains 117
There Is A Dark Spot In The Twilight 118
In The Skies Of Heaven A Noble Eagle Soars ... 120
Another Moment 121
Beyond The Sound Of Waves 122
Sweet Dreams 123
The Gentle Days Of Autumn 124

Realities

Again 126
If I Were 127
If Love Were 128
In Passing 129
In A Padded Room 130
*The Giver And The Taker Come
    To See The Clown's Rose Fall* 132
I Saw You In A Photo 134
Carousel 134
The Spider And The Wasp 135
A Fan Walked Its Wind 136
Concerto Of The Pen In Ink Minor 138
Without Mercy 139

– Table of Contents –

Beyond The Length Of This Reach	140
Once Spoken	142
To These Ends	143
Unity Of Loneliness	144
The Last Love Letter I'll Ever Write (To You)	146
Forever Searching	147
In The Flirt Chatroom	148
When	150
I Thought	151
Golden Words	152
On The Death Of Her Father	154
The Last Parade	156
Museum Of The Dead	157
In The Breath Of Music	158
Without Term	159
Solus	160
Shackled	161
Listen To The Violins	162
Unended	163
In The Passing Of Breaths	164
Wheels On A Cloud	165
Tony Spivey Biography	167
Index	169

ACKNOWLEDGMENTS

With heartfelt appreciation, I would like to personally thank the following people for their contributions to my poetic endeavors.

Leon and Sondra Schlossberg
Sylvia Gail Sammons Spivey
Yumiko Yamashita Spivey
Jerry Sammons Davis
Miriam Sammons Mincey
Susan "Snow" Totaro
Lisa "Galadrial" Shields
January Grey
Cynthia "Dove" Proctor
Camille Cheek
Judith LaBriola
Bedie Jenkins
Sheri Holstein
Bruce Henderson
J.C. Overgaar
Alanna Webb

and very special recognition to
one of God's angels in the UK

Lady Catherine Anderson

COVERED GROUND

LOOKING BACK

A POET SHOULD NOT DIE UNWRITTEN

If I die tonight, then
I shall surely cry in my grave.
Not for the loss of sunsets
or fresh coffee or coconut,
No, these things shall linger
beyond the days of steps
in memories I have known.
It is the things I never did
nor never knew that will
streak tears like trains
into the dark satin tunnel
of my eternal regret.
And it is panic that wakes me
from this timid slumber
in the darkest hours of flight
to rest my head in sweating hands
that clawed their way out
of the night . . .
A poet should not die unwritten
on the parched pages of verse
where love hovers forever unspent
on a windowless, ebony hearse.
The aging hands of a promised walk
along the shore in the red moonlight
should never touch the dead cold
of lips that loved someone that much.
Memories should know the ages
not dream-built castles of sand.
And I should live just long enough
to know the words of your hand.

Forgotten

These fading images on yellowing paper
conjure up thoughts of simpler times,
now revered in my memory.
Instances devoured by insatiable
appetite of time.
Forever pressed into the infinite
dimensions of space;
behind the mirror of life.
Gone . . . like you now.
Retained in the essence
of we who loved you.
Ours only briefly,
for time is relentless.
It calls us all.
We who are destined
to become a memory
told to generations unborn
and then, forgotten.
Except for a name
on a cold, weathered stone.

ONCE

I once ran in walking shoes
through the walls of rain
that burnt tender kisses
on the heels of my wishes
and I held my thoughts
in gasping gazes
that trembled to breathe
of you.

I once knew the sound of purple
and the taste of mercy on palms
that taught me how to speak
without eyes.

I once dreamed in sleeplessness
watching the replay of beginnings
blurred by the speed of slow motion
as timeless moments ticked away
until tomorrow became forever
and you an obsession once known.

Ceramic Clown

On nights when I watched the world sleep
And guarded you from the moans of ghosts
Who hid in the darkness like fish in the sea
You penned love letters in invisible ink
And mailed silent words to me.

When the cloak of death fluttered around me
Engulfing others in morbid screams at random
Dropping them like targets in a fairground gallery
To the laughter of crowds yearning for prizes
You watched yourself in the house of mirrors.

Each time I reached within myself to hold on
While dueling with the hooded vermin of fear
Claiming a stay of execution as victory
And exhaustion as a reward for the effort
You threw translucent lifelines made of mist.

As others unfurled linen paper surrounding gifts
And gazed upon smiles frozen in color
Scented with the flowers of distant hearts
Signed by the stretched fingers of yearning
You tied yellow bows in your hair and forgot.

When this weary warrior became a crystal soldier
Seeking warm light upon curio shelves
There to be remembered and housed in care
Protected from the children of darkness
You bought a ceramic clown and walked away.

THE VESSEL OF INNOCENCE

He was a trash pile
of discarded headlines,
empty cans of thought,
rotting peels of fruit
eaten by life.

There was no shimmer
in a heart petrified
into rustic disfigurement
whose jagged edges
dug painfully
into every breath taken,
unwillingly.

There was no bloom
in a dirty face
wilting to its root
like a shriveled bud
of un-nurtured promise.

There was no color
in the absence
of sunless hopes
that had been eclipsed
into arctic days and nights
of shivering solitude.

What she saw in his eyes,
sunken to the bottom
of soul's ocean,
he will forever ponder.

Perhaps long ago
forgotten treasures

– The Vessel Of Innocence –

she cast upon
ill fated vessels.

Perhaps redemption
for injustice
parleyed upon
innocence.

Whatever the motive . . .
he felt unworthy.

And still
she gave . . .

She . . .
chipped and polished
away at the morbid edges
of his heart with kindness
conveyed in melodious words,
tender touches, and
glances betook from the gallery
of angels.

She . . .
watered and fed
with forgiveness and understanding
until the dried and cracked soil
that once held one willing
thank you, reserved
for the pleasure of death,
became a cathedral of flowers

waking to the prospect
of tomorrow.

– *The Vessel Of Innocence* –

She . . .
painted with brushes
made of her hair,
in hues mixed from the colors
of her eyes, her lips,
her thoughts, and she
unveiled the sun
in the cycle of days
until hope renewed
in the expectations
of starlit nights.

And then,
from the trash pile
he had become,
treasure revealed itself
from within
the open sails
of a vessel . . .
christened by innocence.

His heart
became the emerald
she wears upon her hand.

His smile
became the lilies
that fill their garden.

His love
became the violet sunsets
they watch together
across a tranquil sea.

Too Well

The ornaments of destruction
hung from me
like a bizarre collection
some perverse,
twisted soul
placed hodge-podge
upon a thirsty, withered Christmas tree.
I knew those weapons well.
Too well;
for darkness nor panic
impeded my use of them.
Without hesitation
I used them
time and time again.
Their purpose:
to kill,
to maim,
to leave children
fatherless,
wives; widows,
mothers; empty,
fathers; lonely,
and me alive
to remember . . .
I remember,
too well,
the panic,
the darkness,
the faces.

Old Jill, Dad And Me

As a boy I often wondered
why my dad got up before the dew
to roust about in darkness
like a fumbling shrew.

What in the world was he doing?
What was there to do,
before the day was a day;
before the night was through?

I thought him crazy.
Pure Looney Tunes.
Sleep was too wonderful
to get up so soon.

Why would he leave my mother
to shuffle on cold, wooden floors?
He had to be on a noble quest
or he forgot to do his chores.

He walked with quiet purpose
and design in every step.
A symphony of sound disposed
as about the house he crept.

I would listen to his folly
overt and clandestine.
The echoes I deciphered
were the same every time.

– Old Jill, Dad And Me –

The swallow of a thirsty pot;
the squeak of cupboard's lid;
the chime of a baby spoon;
a search for coffee hid.

He wrestled with the newspaper
and sat on a tired kitchen seat,
while the table creaked and crackled
from the weight of lofted feet.

Soon he would get up again
with a coffee refill in hand
then he'd shuffle to the back porch door
and there he would stand.

He pondered out the window
into the darkness of space,
consumed in the glass pane
that reflected back his face.

I would soon hear old Jill beckon
and dad would don a smile.
He'd slowly step out the door
and then play the porch for awhile.

Old Jill would whine and whimper
until dad gave in
and with a twit and a twitter
he'd unlock her dog pen.

– Old Jill, Dad And Me –

With mocking tones of romance
he would cuddle her lemon fleece
and she would doggy dance
my dad down to his knees.

They would race back to the porch
and settle in gratitude.
Wrapped in each other's solace,
their friendship now renewed.

I knew all of this
from strictly overhear.
What happened after that
still wasn't very clear.

So I joined them one morning
to see with my own sight
and I came to realize
why they watched the end of night.

In the arms of my dad
with old Jill laying under,
I watched as the world blossomed
in wonders un-slumbered.

The breeze brought virgin scents
of honeysuckle and jasper.
Tickled by the bird's wings,
the sky giggled in colors of laughter.

– Old Jill, Dad And Me –

None were closer
than old Jill, dad and me
on those bronzed mornings
I would make a duo three.

We shared many mornings
over the years lived away
and misplaced all our youths
in those fossiled days.

Old Jill is long since gone
and my dad is tired and gray
but I am up every dawn
to welcome another day.

And as the sun awakens
I sit here in memory
casting three long shadows;
Old Jill, my dad and me.

THE VIOLETS OF OUR YOUTH

They were waiting there, remember?
Hiding in the violets
clustered in the green, clover field
where we became lovers.

Love's Whispers.

There we lay searching for luck
while the cool blades of grass
cut the stifling heat of summer.

Darting here and there,
teasing our hearts,
they danced along on the summer breezes.
Each little fairy pausing in turn
to tickle our bare feet.
Our bodies giggled inside and outside
and upside the clouds smiled
from blue to blue.

Love's Whispers.

Jealous of our bond, the sun cast shadows
down upon us
but the fairies carried them away
and, you and I,
laughed until we cried.

Love's Whispers.

– The Violets Of Our Youth –

Searching for the memories long lived away
I went back there today.
The clover field is hidden by yellow weeds;
but there, underneath time,
I found a single violet
glistening in the dew of morning
and I giggled inside and outside
and upside
the clouds
        drifted
                away.

Love's Whispers.

The violet stands out
against the cool, white stone
that cuts the heat of summer
and the sun casts shadows
down upon us.
You and I.

I Don't Know

I don't know where you are.
Memories beg me to search but
I don't know where to look.
If there is a beyond after this life
I don't know where I will go
but I know the truth
will go with me.
Harbored thoughts left
unspoken, known
only to you and to me
do not dissolve
their existence.
What is . . . is.
I don't know how to lie
to myself.
The time we spent together
did not give us meaning.
We gave meaning
to the time spent.
Treasures
I don't know
how to give away.

– I Don't Know –

Somewhere, out there
perhaps you remember
how the touch of your hand
made me feel.
How the smell of your hair
made me breathe.
How the look in your eyes
made me see.
How the sound of your voice
made me hear.
Tonight, I long to feel,
to breathe, to see . . . to hear.
The clock grows weary.
I don't know how
to break the silence.
I don't know how
To say good-bye.

OH, HOW I LOVED YOU

I walked alone
in this daisy field
the day before I left
to hide myself
beneath the green stems
and think of you.

And there I counted
yellow petals of loves me
and loves me not
until the sky turned
grey and it rained.

Oh, how I loved you
But . . .

You were only sixteen
and I a number
whose name had been
called to distant shores.

And you in your youth
with eyes of sapphire flame
and lips of red cotton
yearning to be touched
by more than a ghost.

– Oh, How I Loved You –

The days were lonely and sad
across the cold, blue ocean
where I hid myself
beneath bamboo shoots
and thought of you.

And there I counted
yellow bullets of loves me
and loves me not
until the sky turned
grey and it rained.

Oh, how I loved you.
But . . .

You were only sixteen
with eyes of sapphire flame
and lips of red cotton
yearning to be touched
by more than a ghost.

All I Ever Wanted To Do . . .

when you

>turned my head
>from across that crowded room

>of lonely people,

>washed your hair
>in the summer rain
>of an Appalachian morning,

>talked to me of Venus and Mars
>through the floating light of
>evening candles,

>laughed 'til you peed your pants
>at my momentary regressions
>to adolescent silliness,

>smiled
>in breathless silence when I read
>to you the thoughts I penned
>while you slept,

>touched
>me slowly in the moonlight
>with trembling finger tips,

– All I Ever Wanted To Do –

      dreamed
      while curled up
      in the sleep of my arms,

      waved farewell
      over my shrinking reflection
      in the rearview mirror of that
      old, dusty car,

was love you
with all of my heart.

When We Loved Each Other

We drew starlight peace symbols
on the inside of the backseat windows
and talked of great places
we would someday visit
and kissed until our lips
hurt too good to stop.

Then giggled on the dash
from the car to the house
dancing in the yellow light
of a bug laden porch;
holding each other
wrapped in an old, cotton
blanket you always carried
on our dates in winter
until your mother
used Morse Code
with the light switch
telling us to come in
out of the cold.

– When We Loved Each Other –

Where we made a fire
in the shadows
of black and white movies
unscrambled on late night TV
and sat uncomfortably apart
on the couch
until "mom" went to bed.

Leaving us to tremble
until your brown eyes
and these blue eyes
outlasted the eyes
of the night.

Morning came too quickly
when we loved each other.

A Cry Of Understanding

The red words jagged across your wrist
seeped deep into the white plaster
that fills the cracks in my heart.
And I fell like the tears from your eyes
into a cry of understanding.
Not wanting to live anymore
is a desperation beyond sadness
that dangles around the neck of night
like an empty locket.
Yet, your life is worth more than any
shimmering metal that might hold
an instant in time next to the rise
of breaths to breathe the scent of death.
I felt you tremble in my restless sleep
waking wide eyed in the darkness
I reached across the distance to keep
you from killing another part of me.
Time tethered a bridge across our lives
so that my purpose might meet yours
along our paths to knowing compassion
as the companion of love for another
just because they are who they are.
In these many months of quiet knowing
the red words have faded from your wrist
and laughter now fills that once empty locket.
And that day, as we parted along the tethered bridge
walking in the mist of looking back
I fell like the tears from your eyes
into a cry of understanding.

How Could It Be . . . ?

How could it be
that such wants and wishes
could dissolve upon the ground
like the fallen red bird?

Heart feathers
left, not to taste the sky
but to drift upon the whims
of selfish winds,
in hunger.

How could it be
that serenades of dusk and dawn
could rise above your hearing
like the voice of a cloud?

Majestic songs held in silence
among the trampled leaves
that once rejoiced
on a now armless tree.

Was not the blood of my breast
red enough to paint your talons?

Oh, my beloved long flown away
I could not have loved you more.

Dance Of The Hummingbirds In June

Distance is my winter . . .
and even the flowers cry.
For sorrow falls the brightest petals
with the laughter of madness
even on the most lovely of nights.

A voice glides its way through
the shadow makers in the market.

"Je serai a la maison au printemps . . .
meme le cri de fluers."
And I breathe deep the night.

I remember the whistle of wild roses at dawn
calling you to our white window frame
that they might look upon woman painted
and bloom in the echo of your beauty.

Beauty that falls long like black waters
of ebony silk across fawn shoulders
softer than the cotton grass pining
for the yellow kiss of morning.

I remember you gathering color in a basket
while purple violets sighed blue in the meadow
until they filled the sky with my eyes
and all the world watched you waltz with the wind.

Wind that carried the tune of the trumpet creeper
to every corner of the pale morning moon
until the lullaby of orange too sweet to forget
passed night into the song of sleep.

– Dance Of The Hummingbirds In June –

I remember the restlessness of afternoon
underneath two oak trees on the hill
when long shadows kissed blue-eyed Mary
in the dance of hummingbirds in June.

June more May than peppered July
more timeless than the salt of your voice
spreading across the feast of our love
when we picnicked in the white sand.

I remember you saying, "The sky is a garden on fire;
azaleas hanging against the wall of night."
And the breeze was a perfume of flowers
that you planted to grow in my soul.

A voice glides its way through
the shadow makers in the market.
"Je serai a la maison au printemps . . .
meme le cri de fluers."
And I breathe deep the night.

** "Je serai a la maison au printemps . . .
meme le cri de fluers."

I will be home in the Spring . . .
even the flowers cry.

Mr. Adelson Speaks To My Love
In The Park

Some things transcend time and space.
Some things are meant to be a mystery.

I have known the man you come to sit here with
since he sat upon that bench, his legs too short
to take his little feet down to the ground.

His mother, a beautiful young woman, just as you
looked upon him with the same glow and gleam
as I can see here now in your eyes.

His childish laughter once echoed across this green
like the footsteps of God's gentle forest creatures.
He was a lovely child. He grew into a lovely man.

Sorrow sat there with him for awhile, in sun,
in snow, and in darkness. Even these flowers
I give you now could not brighten this park
when loneliness came to hold his hand.

Everyone here knows him but no one here knew
him way back in those days . . . except perhaps
for you and me, each in our own magic way.

It is you that brought him to sit here again.
Returned from a great and distant slumber
and he blooms like azaleas in spring every time
your shadow crosses his under the mid day sun.

You carry all time that ever passed here;
all the moments yet to come hide in your thoughts;
your hands have the power to rewrite his history.
Even I could swear that it was you as a girl

– Mr. Adelson Speaks To My Love In The Park –

that gave him his very first kiss, there . . .
underneath that wild old, shedding tree.

It was surely your initials he carved with intent
into the wood of these four legged benches
when his hair was fair, full and free.

It was the length of your silhouette he painted
on page after page of tempest white canvas
when he sat here from dawn until dusk.

And the many times that far away took him
from us it was you who sat here and read
the letters he wrote in an ache to come back
home to be here with us again.

 It was you who used to hold him when
he remembered too clearly their faces and you
who knew he came here to hide his cries
while sitting malcontent there in the rains.

It must have been you he wrote the poems for
until blood poured from his pen and passion
screamed across the ages to be named.

It is you who surely wears the ring of his soul.
You are the mother of all the children
that ever lived deep in his heart.

He loved you before you were born dear.
He loved you all the days of his life.
He loves you now more than ever before.

Yes, I have known this man you come to sit here with
since long before we died.

Driftwood And Sea Foam

Driftwood and sea foam
left here on the shore of hearts
where young footsteps pass
into the tempered crash of the sea.

Remnants of a passionate voyage
on a bastion of bowed rapture
with unfurled sails that urged us on
to touch the face of the moon.

Silence In The Wood

remember when I dug your name
into the heart of a tree
so far the tree cried from the pain

the tree grew, taking your name
upwards toward the clouds
far beyond my reach

and there it scarred over
from lack of being traced
until it disappeared

but the tree's heart still ached
from the bleeding inside
and it died from memories

then crashed down to its roots
where it slowly rotted away
into silence . . .

THAT DAY

In that instant, that moment, that day
was the only absolute truth I have ever known.
Far over the curve of the oceans
I traveled to see beauty in hopeless efforts
that I might reframe its meaning
and forever hide you behind those images.
Black and white ones that would not breathe
on my face in the casket of sleep
nor move about my mind like gypsies
lighting fires that burnt my heart to cinders.
I looked upon all of God's earthly wonders
and wondered of all the earthly Gods.
Always pleading that I may be made to forget
and yet forced to remember in each plea.
No color could I find that did not repaint you.
No morning did I wake that left you in a dream.
No jewel did I find that paled the ring of your eyes;
No cloth as soft as the sinful curve of your neck;
No fruit as sweet as the pulp of your tongue;
No quiet as soothing as the sound of your sleep;
No tree as caressing as your hands.
And I looked on and on across the seas.
Days turned to weeks that turned to years
and said, "there is nowhere else for us to go."
And no door did ever I find to a room without you.
The only absolute truth that I have ever known
came in a moment, an instant, that day.

Dead Stars

There was an instant
in the infinity of time
when we illuminated the night
with the spectral effervescence
of a nebula.
We were boiling clouds of passion
entwined in a thunderous dance
of charged particles;
sparkling deliverance beyond
confines and limitations of mortality
into the ethereal bliss
of eternity.
Certain we would shine in unison
fueled by lust and desire
until all that we were returned
to all that we would become
in lives yet to be lived.
Now we hover in the cold
space between us.
Two dead stars
collapsing upon ourselves;
rolling restlessly
searching across a Universe
for the light we once were.

HERE AND NOW

Covered Ground

The seven colors of love arched the valley
with reaching fingers of infinite desire
for more time to cross the sacred mountains
and touch the face of the south China Sea.

But the rainbow ended in the dark clouds
that rolled impatient across the yearning sky.
And rain fell too heavy to carry the light
of our hearts beyond the wet of covered ground.

The double shadow of the black panther
silently cast themselves against the wind
then disappeared into the sighs of wishes we
left abandoned at the doorway of chance.

Now, agony stretches like cobwebs from dream to dream
catching memories on the path of walking death
where the seven colors of love sparkle in the drops
of tears we left puddled in the footprints of then.

Tamed

I gaze upon your beauty
from behind these wires
yearning to reach through
and touch the vivid colors
of your feathers.

I look with desire deep
into the dark eyes of wildness
which glisten in the sunlight.

You are aware of me,
I know,
but you remain wary,
safe in the distance
between us.

With fluttering wings
you offer the promise
of nights circling
moonlit clouds.

But I am too weak,
and afraid to soar
amidst the starlight
on these withering pinions.

Left breathless,
as you take wing,
my eyes follow you
until I see only the wire
which keeps me caged
and an empty sky
where I long to fly.

THIS MORNING, I JUST WATCHED YOU SLEEP

There is a silence at the unfold of day
Like no other I have known.
The breeze is soft, cool and fresh.
The land damp with renewal.
Creatures of the darkness wane
As those of the light awaken.
The transition is peaceful,
Like the eerie calm after battle.

The curtains flutter helplessly
In the breath of morning,
As do the stray strands of your hair.
You lay naked, motionless,
Except for the slow rise and fall of your breasts,
Curled up as though reaching with your whole body
Across the room for me.

I indulge myself to savor every inch of you.
My eyes making love to you in the silence.
The sheets transform from gray to white,
As the mirror reveals its first reflection.
Me sitting in this chair.

– This Morning, I Just Watched You Sleep –

In distance there is a fondness
That fills me like the light slowly filling this room.
It comes from a place so far within myself
That I cannot get there alone.
It is you who takes me there
When you say my name in the quivers of passion.
When you smile just because I'm here.

Painters and poets, musicians and composers
Throughout the epic of time
Have tried to capture love in an image
A sound, a word, a rhyme.
Men of prominence and paupers
Have tried to convey it
In life and to the death.

This morning, I just watched you sleep.

Love Verse

I do not love you like spring does the dove
nor fireflies the dimming cloak of the dusk.
I do not love you like a mother's love
nor the guarding hugs of corn by their husk.

I love you like the winter's piercing winds
that seek warmth swirling through unseen places.
I love you like the river's changing bend
that carves harshly into rocky faces.

I do not love you like a ship on the sea.
I love you like honey does the honey bee.

Until Time Bows Me Old

Wear me like thin, faded jeans
soft against pampered skin.
Wash me like dirty dishes
and put me up again.

Wrap me like fountain wishes
under ripples of dreams.
Wreak me like vengeance does peace
to the murdered last screams.

Weave me like a winding road
cut through the hills of your soul.
Weather me like sun dried wood
until time bows me old.

Your Hands

How warm your hands are
curling against my face
like the first grateful clutch
of morning coffee
and I need look no deeper
than the brown of your eyes
for the sacred meanings of life.

Perhaps the great maker
pardons us, in these moments,
for the markers of our sins
that we may carry into eternity
the nakedness of truth.

Timelessness has no bounds
nor the depth of contentment
that your hands imprint
within the sands of my days.

And no breath shall I take
less than the shadow of your words,
no vision shall I make
less than the light of your smile.

No sleep shall I slumber
neath the wings of tomorrow
in this life or the rest
without the curl of your hands.

The Moaning Well

Waking here inside the gazebo
hidden deep within the vines
of the garden
I realize that many seasons
have been spent in dreadful slumber
while under the spell
of an overdose
of heartache.
And the many years we walked
these flowered paths
hath been but dreams
of long ago footsteps
crisscrossing patterns
where once we chased
each other's hearts.

There is no scent of the perfume
that once lingered in my every thought
and flamed every passionate kiss.
There is only the stench of decaying
flowers and dreary green antiquity
that covers the lily pond in sadness.

The towers that held golden gates
now stoop like old men in the rain.

The white marble wishing well
where we paid for happiness
sits disabled and worn
down to crumbling sandstone
with parched lips chaffed by the winds.

Winds that once made your hair dance,
taunted butterflies and tickled fall leaves.

– The Moaning Well –

Winds that moan from the mouth
of the well, like a great horn
pointing toward the Heavens
holding an infinite note of agony.

I am drawn to the well
as if dying of thirst, yet
it is not water that I crave.

It is the deep darkness
beneath these haunting memories
of a once floral paradise
shared with you,
that beacons my sorrow
to drown itself and rest
amid the tokens of love
we tossed so carelessly away.

Conjuring forth every ounce
of longing for you that festers
inside of me like infected wounds
I moan in harmony with the keeper
of sorrow until the sounds flow
through me as if they were my blood
and I lean over the jagged edges
of the watery soul of the oracle
to take leave of this purgatory.

Only to find myself looking up
from the bottom of the moaning well.

I'm Leaving

Don't ask me to wait.
Don't ask me to stay.

I'm leaving.

I ripped away
all the layers of protection
that surrounded me, and
stood before you
as vulnerable as a peeled orange.
You . . .

You squeezed tighter and tighter
until the fluids which kept me
a sphere
of blissful contentment
ran down your arm, and
dripped, drop by drop,
into a disgusting array
of agony
clinging to the floor
of this apartment.
You . . .

You threw away the pulp, and
all the seeds, except one,
which you left
to dry up and waste away
in the harsh loneliness
of being taken for granted.

Don't ask me to wait.
Don't ask me to stay.

I'm leaving.

– I'm Leaving –

I'm going to search
for a place to replant
in hopes, with time,
I will once again grow
into an orange,
round and whole.
And maybe,
find someone
who will nurture that fragility.

Don't ask me to wait.
Don't ask me to stay.

I'm leaving.

I'm going before I rot
away into oblivion,
alone in a corner,
becoming nothing
more than someone
who once was
very much in love with you.

Don't ask me to wait.
Don't ask me to stay.

I'm leaving.

On Highway 43

The road curves like
red wigglers.
Green caterpillars crawl
from the fields
ridden by parched men
with droopy pants
and beer guts.
College girls weave
elaborate patterns
across the yellow lines
while painting faces
on hangovers
in oblong mirrors.
Dead flowers on white crosses
dot the roadside
like an old summer dress.
Wrinkled ladies grasp
ironed housecoats
in feeble hands
at mailboxes too close
to the way east.
Gray remnants of posterity
gaze upon the procession
through broken glasses
and hollow eyes.
Watching the early bird
get the worm
on highway 43.

I Love You . . .

Beyond the confines of my heart
into the landscape of my soul
where the hills and the valleys meet
to transcend the young into the old

On the seashores and mountain tops
where the white caps dance in the wind
and in the brooks, and creeks, and rivers
that flow to the memories of old friends

In the trees and the flowers of gardens
planted in dream tilled sod
that give birth to prayerful wishes
in the whispers of the angels of God

Over the oceans and under the seas
traversing the tides of the moon
that guide by night amorous sails
filled with the song of the loon

Eternally into the infinite night
speckled with celestial paint
on a canvas of endless tomorrows
hanging on heaven's gate

Passing Time At The China Doll

A blue neon nymph dances
in mid air above cracked streets
where loneliness hunts her prey
from the inside of empty fifths
strewn about like discarded clothes
on the filthy floors of seedy hotels
which line the midway of flesh

The door reads you're welcome
as if to concede itself to pleasure
given in the dark corners
below hanging boxes of noise
which mute the moans of release
from another night's frustration
in sweaty moth-eaten sheets

Faces turn briefly to look
for a face misplaced somewhere
in the pockets of discarded clothes
worn to meetings of forgiveness
with strangers who could care less
about salvation or redemption
for the sins necessary to forget

Cold beer foams at the mouth
of bottomless mugs
that leave wet circles of thought
around carved initials in tables
holding chins off of the floor
beneath shoes worn too thin
from sand-dancing alone

– Passing Time At The China Doll –

You tower above the conclave
of worshipers at your feet
adorned in golden high heels
that change color with the light
spotting stacks of broken bills
folded into half inch strips
of restless appreciation

We talk between sets alone
with the ire of a hundred eyes
peering into the conversation
of places you would like to see
beyond the confines of reality
where you can waltz to music
played by a lover's hand

The sunrise hides the nymph
within the broken background
of the China Doll sign
hanging over the hungry smiles
we paint below glazed looks
as we drift apart toward sleep
in beds made for two

ON A GRAY, DUSTY WALL

She sits alone,
in a room made for two,
staring into yesterday,
dressed in white
and not enough make-up
to hide her age,
though she tried.
Tears wait tenuously
in her eyes
to fall without warning.
She hums a song.
The words long forgotten
but the dance preserved
in black and white grains
of silver.
Trembling hands hold
a monogrammed handkerchief
worn thin by searching fingers
and she dances
in whirling swirls of happiness
while seated
in a fragile pose
of reflection,
oblivious to the silence
of outliving life.
Content to wait for death
remembering
the moments captured
in ten faded pictures
on a gray, dusty wall.

The Silence Of Alone

3 A.M.
shadows dance
on deaf walls
heartbeats
echo
in hollow chambers
muted
by the thinness
of a plastic pillow
inadequate comfort
for nocturnal cravings
breathing
becomes willed labor
covering the portal
to dreamless sleep
agony hangs
like wet hair
over bloodshot eyes
blinded by the silence
of alone

As If

I can feel the craving desire
you have to find a place
of peace and love
within the arms of a savior
as if you were one
of the contorted souls adrift
on the Raft of the Medusa.

I can hear the sobs of fear
you muffle with shaking hands
while looking into the face
of loneliness peering
over trembling shoulders
struggling for possession
of clutched sanity
as if you were living
a Death and the Mother.

I can taste the bittersweet
nectar and salty sweat
left on wandering hands
driven by colorful fantasies
appearing in the darkness
behind tightly closed eyes
unwilling to become
The Blind Man's Meal.

– As If –

If I could somehow
transform my spirit into
the nebula's spirit of a ghost
I would transcend time and space
and arrive with quiet purpose
upon your bedside
as if I were kneeling
in The Adoration of the Shepherds.

I would lick the nectar
from your fingers and dry
the tears of yearning
falling from your closed eyes
and open them to my own
while vaulting you into
the bittersweet mist
of ecstasy somewhere
in the Starry Night.

In The Rain

Outside the sky plays patty-cake
with its sibling ground
and everywhere that I look
there are pools of play to be found.
I want to hide these aged lines
in the childish wrinkles of play.
I want to laugh at absolutely nothing
and remember my youthful days.
What I was called as a boy
is still my name.
It is as old as I am
but it did not change.
Somewhere deep inside of me
that little boy remains
and today we are going outside
just to play in the rain.

Just For You

If my heart were a door
to a room of comfort and rest
where your face could glow in a smile,
I would leave it unlocked
With a welcome sign upon it
in hopes you would stay there awhile.
And in your stay, I would pray
in thanks to our God above
for the blessing each day
and the chance to say,
it is you that I dearly love.

I Ache

I ache to rise, higher and higher,
above your horizon
like the sun in the morning sky.
I ache to alight softly upon your petals
like the bumble bee and taste
the flavor of your nectar.
I ache to softly glide across the tips
of your mountains
like the tongue of a cloud.
I ache to make ripples
upon your calm waters
like the wind upon a lake.
I ache to make you sing
like the dusk does to a nightingale.
I ache to fall over your edge
like the waterfall does the cliff.
I ache to crash, again and again,
into your cove
like the waves of a tidal ocean.
I ache to cover your land
like the volcano's lava eruption.
I ache to slowly set
over your horizon
like the sun in a purple sky.

3 A.M. At The Veterans Hospital

Dark shadows dance upon
the bright white walls
of the corridors,
defying the laws of gravity.
They giggle like children
playing hide and seek
as they dart in and out
of the cracks in the mortar
and through the lines
on the speckled, tile floor.
Whispering obscenities in anger
for having died alone,
in obscurity,
forgotten.
Their silhouettes show
no signs of the arms
and legs left behind,
buried in distant places . . .
I study each figure
as I walk the long walk
to the smoking pit.
Making sure your shadow
does not descend
from the eighth floor
in my selfish absence
and I read every word
on every locked door,
count every spot on the floor,
wondering who bled life there,
and I listen
to the silence.

– 3 A.M. At The Veterans Hospital –

The translucent gateway to the outside
opens magically
as I approach.
Somehow it knows
I am one of the living,
and the shadows that hawk me
recede into the walls,
afraid of the bitter cold.
It reminds them of death.
I sit in a soliloquy
on a frosted wooden bench,
spotlighted by the red glow
of an inadequate heat lamp,
like a day old hamburger
thinly wrapped and stale
in some off-beaten fast food chain.
Waiting . . .
The heat lamp, tired of fighting
the overwhelming odds of winter,
clicks off.
Leaving me to shiver as I fill my lungs
with the smoke
of two cigarettes
chained until the stench of burning filter
permeates the condensed exhales
of distorted circles.
Without warning
panic descends upon me
like the darkness of 3 A.M.
I need to be on the eighth floor,
behind the restricted entrance
to intensive care.

– 3 A.M. At The Veterans Hospital –

I need to make sure
all twenty-one life lines
keeping you from becoming a shadow
are imbedded deep in your skin
like ticks.
I need to hear the beep, beep, beep,
of your heartbeat.
I need to hold your hand.
I need to watch you breathe.
I study each figure
as I walk the long walk
back from the smoking pit.
Making sure your shadow
does not descend
from the eighth floor
in my selfish absence
and I read every word
on every locked door,
count every spot on the floor,
wondering who bled life there,
and I listen
to the silence.

The Peep Hole

Dark curtains
shield the outside view
from the inside
hiding secrets
in dim light
where you hide
underneath a bed
heart bleeding
in undecorated hues
of insanity.
Words echo
in muffled speech
quietly forced
through a chained passage.
One blood
shot eye
cried red
from blue
stares through
the peep hole
into distant
places
somewhere
behind my face.
Told to go away
by frightened pleas
that unconsciously begged me
to stay
you left me standing.
The door looking at me
and I peeping into its soul.

First Kiss

I forget to breathe
as all my years
condense
into a single need
and all the passion
long stored away
exults
in being freed
by the fire
in your hair
and the sky
in your eyes
and the taste
of wine
on your lips
as they press
against mine
forever in time
in love
from the very
first kiss

Under The Glow Of The Moon

Late at night when ghosts appear
in every mirror, front and rear,
we share the confines of shadowed space
hidden in our parking place
under the glow of the moon.

As breaths escape each unlocked kiss
tangled hands become one fist,
passion stops to roll a laugh
in panting sighs of aftermath
under the glow of the moon.

Head to breast
there we rest
arms entwined
yours and mine
under the glow of the moon.

Quantum Kisses In The Ethereal Garden

~ Prelude: Voices They Cannot Hear ~

Eternal things are not of this world.
So say the muses beneath hearing.
The Angels sing only in Heaven.
So say the ghosts beneath fearing.

Seven steps up the mountain to the promised land;
somewhere across the lakes of regret –
Perhaps on the ledges of lesser heights
the poets and teachers gather wet . . . to write.

Even the virgins bleed
the crippled seed
and the mindless weed
grows tall . . .
enough to obscure reality
from a man lost
in his dreams.

~ Stave One: Epiphany in the Meadow ~

Dainty white flowers without a name
turned into love me knots
that tied me to the ground
that I might see blue in a lighter shade
surrounding the dance of your hair.
Hair of copper wisps, fingers of the breeze,
that played my face like a game.

– Quantum Kisses In The Ethereal Garden –

The meadow rose opened wide to see
why the sparrows would not wing
and the secret song of the bumblebee
crossed the lips of our hearts to sing.

I did not know of the empty place –
before the rains of the fall.
And that winter I was never cold,
never cold at all . . .

It was winter –
that winter the universe condensed
into the amber sky of your eyes
and your name rang out in the meadow
just because it tickled my ears
and you were the laughter
of all my days . . .
of all of my days,
my dear.

I came to know why the old man died
crumpled, alone on the iron rod bench . . .
the one no one knew
but the lover gone
on the meadow song
of sparrows that took wing.

I came to know there was an empty place
because you filled it with the pour of your touch.

I came to know of heartbreak
and slow death by the meadow brook.

~ Stave Two: Cacophony of the Meadow Crow ~

The cold, black brook chases itself
in fleeting fury
refusing to be contained, held, or admired
for more than an instant.
Its liquid babble beating smooth the rock
into slimy stone.
Cutting out the virgin earth
to uproot the meadow rose.
Loud and louder and louder still
the water's feet
stomp away running . . .
chasing the sparrow to the sea
taking the pour of you in me
in each gulp of the thirsty crow.

And the meadow weeds hide
the bumblebee's secret . . .
the shade is thick on the bench
where the young man grows . . .
grows and grows
grows and grows
old.

And you are the laughter of days . . .
all of my days
all of my days,
my dear.

~ Stave Three: Lament of the Sparrow ~

The bark of the dogwood never ceases
to cover the silence of your initials in the tree
and my knuckles bleed trying to find
a migrant path . . . out of my mind.

But they would have me shackled in silver rings
that promise no certainty of ever healing . . .
just patching wounds that scar deeper
with every turn of the lock and key.

And the moonlight crawls too slowly
underneath the chamber door.

I need no sleep; I need no food.
I need to know the whys.
I need no sleep; I need no food.
I need to say good-byes.

The rainbow is a jagged crown
that obscures too many distant clouds . . .
The rain makes mud cries out of dirt pain
and the brook babbles loud and loud
and LOUD.

Oh, gracious host of the land of ghosts
she could not see the eagle in my sparrow wings
and thus, I must, I must in trust
confess . . . that I will die
never having learned to fly.

~ Stave Four: Vespers at the Zephyr of Dusk ~

We gather here to lay down forever
the old man that no one knew
and here we place a meadow rose
among the white flowers that have no name.

Let the babbling brook give him cool drink for his thirst;
let the scarred tree give him shadow for his sleep;
let the ground be a warm blanket in the cold winter;

and let the silence here be a restful peace
from the torturing rains of the fall.

~ Codicil: In the Meadow ~

And your name rings out in the meadow
just because it tickles my ears
and you are the laughter
of all my days . . .
of all of my days,
of all of my days
my dear.

TANGLED HEART STRINGS

The swing slows to stillness
amid the glittering fortune of this
treasured moment spent with you

until we sit bathed in the dimming
light of another afternoon's fade
to places beneath toe marks in the sand.

In the awkward silence of our quiet
gathering of thoughts I am escorted
once again to the temple of declaration.

And so many times afore I have wavered
succumbing to the weakness of indecision
leaving us dangling on tangled heart strings.

This day as I sit upon the precipice
that leads friends onto the stage of lovers
let me untangle the strings of this heart's puppet
and place them gently within your hands.

Secret Love

I am afraid to walk upon the shards
of broken hearts and thus silence
falls upon me like the dust of antiquity.

Damp and shivering, this soul huddles
around flickering flames rising with doubt
from the ashes of dreams I let fade.

And yet, I cannot muffle these thoughts
nor bridle the wild winds of love
that whistle through my mind.

I cannot keep this secret from myself.
I can only disguise it in your presence
beneath laughter and distance.

Your Embrace

I covet not thy open space
nor seek to follow a bloodless trace.
I merely wish to touch your face
forever in this flowered place.

Where wrongs by right are displaced
and love makes way with all due haste
in each moment shared not to waste
within the shelter of your embrace.

BLACK RAIN

These eyes have seen creation and death.
They have laid upon smiles and cried.
They have seen sunsets over oceans
And lights dancing beyond the clouds.
They have seen shadows in the darkness
And darkness casting shadows in the Light.
They have read words beyond understanding
And understood art beyond any words.
They have closed to sleep in uneasy rest
And rested easy to awaken once again.
They have spoken in the language of souls
And translated another's soul unspoken.
They have uncovered mysteries in the clouds
And unclouded the mystery of cover.
They have quenched the thirst of desire
And lay thirsty upon the walls of loneliness.
They have fed my mind with life's knowledge
And consumed beauty with gluttonous abandon.
Now they sit weary and besieged
By a great dread come to take them away.
And each glimpse now takes on priceless worth
In the museum of my mind's recall.
Left there to please these sightless eyes
While I listen to the pounding black rain.

When I Sit Silently Beside You

In my muted contentment
there are no secrets seething
beneath the voiceless thoughts
there are only truths and dreams.

And if I were to write them down
or whisper them unto your
eyes and ears, would they not
become more yours and less mine?

Would they not be like strangers
who you once smiled at in passing
and then forgot or would they frame
themselves on the wall of your heart?

There for me to meld with in reflection
or not there for me to ever know
in my muted contentment
where there are no secrets seething.

Beneath the voiceless thoughts
there are only truths and dreams
strangers passing and smiling
at the frames of you in my heart.

Windless Chimes

When the night
dresses herself
in wear of sparkles
that serenade
the waning moon,
I listen
and remember
the way
you once sang
that lover's tune.
The one
that comes from
teardrop stains
rolling down
the turn of time
to wet
the fingertips
of forever
as they play
on windless chimes.

Toothpaste And Underwear

I am not sure how far
two bologna sandwiches
will take me . . .
It is a long way
to nowhere.

I used to feel my wallet
when I sat down
for a long time.
Now I just feel
the springs in this seat.

I smell musty socks,
diesel fuel and cigar smoke
mixed with stale cologne
and still underneath
body odor drifts outward
from the fat lady
with the straw, flowered hat
sitting up front.
Only the bus driver can't
smell it. He has AC.

Few people talk.
No one seems to care
to listen.
They just keep posing
as if someone were painting
the thousand words
of despair.

A most beautiful young woman
with wild brown hair
and wild child eyes

– Toothpaste And Underwear –

huddles in the seats
just across the aisle
clinging tightly
to an oversized purse . . .
startled to panic
with each loud whoosh
of the air brakes.

My God,
how I would love
to talk to her.
How I would talk
to love her . . .
were I not ashamed
of myself.

I wonder if her grandmother
said good-bye
giving her that ugly purse
and maybe, bologna sandwiches
while reminding her
to brush her teeth
and wear clean underwear
just in case . . .

Shadow Dancing

The music lifts me to the floor
on the melody of remembered notes
that we wrote our own words to
in between kisses and touches
and laughter.
The candle's flame dances with me
in the recollection of shadows
that once painted these walls
with memories.

Touch My Hand That I May See

When the day comes we can no longer walk
and love is made with idle talk
come and sit beside me
near the maple tree
and touch my hand that I may see
the birds sing songs of days gone by
and roses open their eyes to cry
new spring tears in the question why
must we live to merely die?

Quietly Wicked

The frost comes in silence
like the palmless hands of light
to cover her in sparkling cold prisms
of day stars that sigh forever
alone in the torrid night.

The assassin is a shadow
hidden beneath a feeble grin
that curls to catch tear handles
dripping from curved, steel blades
as sharp as voodoo pins.

The darkness is a sadist mask
adorned with studs of bloodstone
carved from the arch of passion
rising over the valley of lust
between together and alone.

The grave is a shameless place
where secrets hang on a dead vine
curled around whispers in the moonlight
over satin sheets forever turned down
for a lover that never was mine.

I Know Her In Words

I know her in words, only words . . .
gathered like flowers for a vase
to grace a polished, ringless table
with eight chairs that never move.

And the song of her heart floats
across the symphony of tempest nights
to shelter the dawning of rebirth
in arms too white to touch death.

Distance is a hollow drain of time
that swallows might-have-beens
into the bowels of sleepless nights
under the scorn of the red moon.

Ah, but the words, the words never rest
and they tempt the legs of a cripple
to run across the meadow in pain
just to know the taste of the wind.

They ring the heart like a wire fence
with no gate from which to flee
thus dig the restless condemned
to find freedom from a life sentence.

I know her in words, only words . . .
falling like snow from a gray sky
to cover the wilted rose garden
in drifts of shredded blank paper.

I know her in words, only words . . .

Tonight

Flowers do not unfurl themselves
to the virgin bee
in the colors that your hands
reveal within the chance
confines of this awakening
tonight.

Sunsets do not drift into ecstasy
behind the heavy eyelids
of day with more passion
than the sound of your voice
into the echoes of my knowing
tonight.

Spring rains do not fall upon
the fevered tongue of the desert
with more compassion
than your desire
upon my need
tonight.

Holding On

On these days
these too short days
that trample me like horses
never clears the obscured trail
twisting into the darkness

Tethered here to long thin lines
of opaque liquid curse
knowing all the while
that death has an unquenched thirst

But still I wrap my spirit's fingers
deep into the vines of clinging
that I might know another moment
of being who I am

The one whose body feels your hands
reaching through your heart
The one whose eyes cry cold tears
knowing we must part

On these days
these too short days
that drain me like streams
never calm the onward flow
fading into endless dreams

– Holding On –

Resting here on soft thin lines
of flowered pastel linen
knowing all the while
that death takes no vacation

But still I sink my spirit's toes
deep into the sands of waiting
that I might know another moment
of being who I am

The one whose body feels your hands
reaching through your heart
The one whose eyes cry cold tears
knowing we must part

Eight Thousand Days

Eight thousand days I have loved you
with the tempest fervor of hot winds
searching across the barren desert
for rain clouds to lift with adoration
until they fell their tears to make a sea.

A sea of ships each mast unfurled
by lover's words set adrift on dreams.

Eight thousand days the winds have howled
across the barren soil and sea
and my lover's words have all fallen thirsty
to die face down a dusty death
of crumpled white bone picked clean.

Brush Strokes

Life
has
become
nothing
more
than
brush strokes
without
paint
on the canvas
that was
you.

First Light Of Day

she playfully tickles
my eyelashes beckoning
me to rise above
the ledge of sleep
and consume her
offerings . . . fresh

yet, this slumber sits
like an over indulgent sow
sunken up to her curly
tail in crusting mud

my brain weary
from transcendent leaps;
tesseracts to impossibility
through the archways
of imagination

my body, a photo,
still in the moment
of knowing her
emptiness . . .

TO STEAL FROM THE DEVIL

Sin is the curve
of your neck as it becomes
shoulders too pale
for my tongue to paint
alone.

Rain could not trace
a more tempting trail
down flesh
and my hands are washed
wet
with each reach
into the Nile
that is your eyes.

And I steal them
in the dim light
that they may look
inside of me
and heal the blisters
of shameless burn
that scar each moment
stolen.

But I would
steal them from the Devil
if it were he who held them.

Without Regret

Pace thyself with me not blindly
nor bound by momentary weakness.
Take this hand to chain us knowing

there will be an inevitable ending
that waits to confront us as if it were
a guard to the sacred venue of plurality.

Somewhere along the shadowed maze
we shall run through panting, always looking back,
over cautious shoulders, with nervous laughter.

And yet, in the hovers of concealed keeps
our secret liaisons will consummate
the offering of hearts to hungered souls.

Giving eternal purpose to the journey.
And should there be a tribunal
at the end of the adventure

that condemns us to wander
within the dark recesses of persecution
let it be a fate foreseen
and accepted without regret.

I Am The Sea

She is the vessel
and her hair the sail
that moves the waves
of my fingers in a rush
from the horizon to the shore
and back again.

She is the sun
and her smile the shine
that drops the clouds
of my eyes to the night's lips
that I might taste her reflection
over and over again.

Blame Me

If rapture evades your longings
like wolves the human scent
stain not the pillow case
with droplets from your heart's woe
blame me
for the hollow touch
of a wandering shadow
blame me
for the perpetual fall
of pale leaves to untravelled paths.

She Is

she is the stretch of morning
that lifts light to the heavens

she is the hand of the wind
that holds birds in the sky

she is a sheet of soft music
that wraps sorrow in comfort

she is the lashes of the moon
that sparkle the night's eyes

she is the veins in green leaves
that pump red into a rose

she is fresh tulip kisses
that taste of summer rain

she is love in bare feet
that arch into rainbows

she is the curve of thunder
that turns clouds into fire

SECRETS SCRIPTED

Feathered hand dances on pale white paper,
secrets scripted in the color of never tell.
Midnight thoughts tossed over the empty side
of magnificent ships that will never sail.

Lighthouse beacon sings bright in the fog,
music played in the tune of never heard.
Morning kisses torn from the tattered book
of old love poems with too many words.

And there . . . yes there, against the shameless sky
flies my love among the hummingbirds
too fast to kiss the coming Spring
And all the taste of sweet violet eyes
are lost in her hovering wings.

The rose nor tulip nor honeysuckle blooms
give paths to the ends of her search.
Where hands dig deep into un-watered soil
to till a house made of root rooms
built for a songbird to perch.

Feathered hand dances on pale white paper,
secrets scripted in the color of gone away.
Midnight dreams slip to the darker side
of endless wakes to these songless days.

BLUE PENNIES DOWN

Hot rain falls like blue pennies down
through the tired glow of the old city
lamps stooping to look quietly over
the red cobblestone streets of the night.

Star gazers and moon watchers line
the wall arms of a concrete guard
guiding the slither of the Savannah River
until it empties its secrets into the sea.

A haunting loneliness peeks out beneath
the dry laughter of street walkers and men
too low on sleep to remember dreams
and too high on white death to count.

And then there are the forgotten ones
who remember more than just names
of the friends and lovers they used to be
to the coin wishers who threw them away.

Hot rain falls like blue pennies down
through the tired glow of the old city
just watching the slither of the Savannah River
empty my secrets into the sea.

My Love Is A Simple Love

My love is a simple love;
not in the way that time
is a simple measure of
passing moments but
more that it is pure and
timeless in its way and
its measure cannot be
ticked away or pointed
out in some number
whose value is more
or less than the sum
of itself and nothing.

My love is a simple love;
more complex than any
meaning of life that you
or I can conjure in words
or deeds or tangible
objects that symbolize
the idea proposed in
religions so profound
that the truth hides under
the purpose of hearts.

My love is a simple love;
poured from the fall of
hair so dark I drink of
liquid sleep through
the tongue of my fingers
and melt as does the winter
snow into the promise of
roses in spring.

THIS LOVE IS NOT MISPLACED

This love is not misplaced
nor unfair.
It is mine
for you.
It is to you and of you.
It is the lark's song
that gives each morning purpose.
It is a barefoot shadow
that knows not its darkness.
It is soft touches
in our passings
across opposite pages
of tethered verse.
It is I who write them
for you to read
and you who ties them
to my fingers
that I should not forget.
This love is not misplaced
nor unfair
it is mine
for you.

Gently

Let rain gather in your hair
that it might fall across soft shoulders
and wash my hungry kisses down
in drops of melting lips
that love you to the bare bottom
of your naked feet.

Let the pure white light of moon
rest to sleep upon fawn curves
that cut woman from the sheets
of red velvet whispers
unfolded.

Let the tick of timeless clock
betray its echo in the dark
and chase our hands in circles
until they turn flesh to fire
burnt sighs.

THE TASTE OF HER SOUL

How am I to kiss lips more luscious than velvet
when they are the mouth of the wind?

How am I to wash golden hair more soft than silk
when it is the morning light of each day?

How am I to know the smell of your body
when it is the scent of every flower unfurled?

How am I to lay closed eyes against your breasts
when they are the waves of every sea?

How am I to capture the restless love of your heart
when it is every bird that fills the sky?

How am I to touch the smooth curves of your body
when they are the heavens of the universe?

How am I to know the taste of your soul
when it is every fruit born on the trees?

Captured

You are as the spider
weaving
tangles to turn my head
sharply as the blade
to fall running under
traps
I can not see
but feel like the skin
of a peach.

All day I pull them
from around me
yet each thread reminds me
of your hair, like brown time
falling from the half glass
in march to a place
where love piles itself
to grow wicked
as the laugh of hyenas
on the savanna.

– *Captured* –

I feel them tie my head
to my feet
until my ears walk
across the sandy wash
and the taste of salt
pleases me
too much
but I am the wave crash
over lips
more violet than ruby
more silk than stone
more you than your shadow
underneath me.

And I say my piece
to place within the puzzle
of your thoughts,
deeper than the gasp
of astonished bystanders,
ticks who suck blood from our moon
in August at the park.

Black Sleep

If I could take the agony
of those days and gather
them like dead leaves
and tie them unseen
deep into a body bag
labeled with a toe tag
for burial at sea
I would but
agony is not a dead thing
it is alive
living inside of walls
pedaling the cycle of the butterfly
to sometimes crawl
insatiably eating
at my peace . . . of mind
until crusting over
into a larva of pain
hanging too high in silence
to cut down
and then . . .
drifting upon the wing
of nightmare winds
to the heart of flowers
in bloom on white markers
growing out of black sleep –
sleep that marks time
in distance from the echoes
of laughter from young faces
that never grow old.

Beyond The Fall

It is sad to be undone
as if the soul were a button
hanging
by one loose red thread
above the distance to black stillness.

But it is always your fingers,
your eyes, your lips
that unclothed me
to walk naked in the fires
of remembering.

Always your sighs
that mold me on a pedaled wheel
where plainness turns
up its nose to guilt and regret.

What would there be
in less of you,
but too much more
of me?

And it is your night song
that threads these eyes
from spools of images
longer than the span of time.

Always your gate
that swings open
one step beyond
the tumble of this fall.

The Procession

The blue shadows of vagabond rain clouds
crawl through the night faded blades
of summer green grass
in a moonlight projection
of the ghostly, wind blown procession
silently taking place
high above my dew dampened hair.
I am spellbound, trying to comprehend
the disappearance
of the gliding, hallowed shadows
into the obscurity
of the distant nocturnal void.
I am disturbed by the dissolving
of such beauty into nothingness.
I try to hold them in place
with the weight of my earthly body
but they slip between
my feet and the Earth, undaunted.
They drift away
toward their impending demise
like soldiers charging certain death.
I sit among them,
hoping by some twist of fate,
I might ride along with them
as if I were on a magic carpet
and I could see, exactly,
where they are so determined to go.
But, they are too weary with travel
to carry me.
So, I look up into the bright white light
and watch the faces of a thousand souls,
smiling, as they pass over me
on their way to eternity.

Rain On The Window

I want to brush aside
the curtain of hair
that hides your face
and lift your eyes to mine
that you may fall
into them and not
over the edge of life.
I want to wipe away
the tears that stream
down your cheeks
like rain on the window.
I reach for you
but my hands touch
only my reflection
in the pane of glass.
I dare not reach
further to scatter
myself into shards
that I may save you.
So I sit looking
at myself on the inside
and you on the outside
weathering the storm
while I catch these fears
in a chalice of wine
where they turn
as red as our blood.

WILD HORSES

The mesa is a spectral fan
of shattered fire
scattered across the face
of rock and sky.

Tumbleweeds run along
with the wind
to find a place of end
where their roots
can grow
if only for the night.

Sundown's blaze turns
to piercing embers
burning in the black depths
of satin space.

And I rest my saddle here
in the sand.

The yellow blaze of tangled fire
reminds me of your hair.
The circle of white desert stones
caress your neck,
in my mind, like pearls.

The flames cut the cold of distance
with sharp moments of warmth
that dart away in an instant
to remind me I am alone.

– Wild Horses –

But sorrow is like my weary horse;
too ready to flee
to buckle his knees
and make sleep prints in the sand.

I guess my love for you is like wild horses
that come like whispers after midnight
from beyond the sacred Comanche stands.

The shadows of ghostly stallions fall from the sky
to drift along through the night with them
and carry the fevered cries of young lovers
lost between this world and the next.

In the black eyes of wildness
are the flickering blue parades of time
where capture is a death
of tormented spirit, eternal.

And I know they are the keepers
of perpetual secrets
no man should ever tell.

Sometimes

sometimes the distance folds me
as if I were a page torn from you
and placed deep in the dark pocket
of a desperate fugitive . . .

all the words hidden to run away
far beyond the story they tell
and the book left missing moments
too far from the end . . .

days become blank paper
crumpled up and thrown at corners
where walls meet to draw lines
that only shadows can cross . . .

nights become black ink
splattered across a white floor
where tiles hold footprints
that come and go to nowhere . . .

sometimes the distance folds me
as if I were a tissue airplane
drifting silently down to stillness
too flimsy to fly across space . . .

sometimes the distance folds me
away inside myself . . .

sometimes the distance folds me

sometimes

ASHES

silhouettes dance against the fire
but shadows don't burn, only souls
and hearts blister from the pain
of kisses from the lips of letting go

laughter curls up into the night
on the deep released sighs of hope
tied to the wishes of one who waits
longer than the distance of memory

even scarred wood will make ashes
that fly out of the eternal flames

and to where do these ashes flee
the paper thin sparks of once were
do they all just drift away cold
or do some become the grey clouds

could it be that old lovers cry in rains
falling from the dirty feet of memories
running across the sun shrouded sky

silhouettes dance against the fire
but shadows don't burn, only souls
and hearts blister from the pain
of kisses from the lips of letting go

Just For Me

The fields are covered with the dying
and the dead, flags flying, in the burning
ruins of a tranquil valley where children
once laughed and ran after their names.

We rest in the arms of victory too feeble
to keep us safe from tomorrow's travail
when the blue masses gather to avail this day
and lay siege to the few of us that remain.

The thought of dying is less frightening
than the unbearable shame of running away
but that recourse develops like the morning
when I contemplate no more wakes with you.

How my hands do tremble to write farewell
when all they long to do is hold you just once more;
to gather your bosom to my weary breast;
to smell love in the colors of your hair.

No moment has passed even in the rage of battle
that your face has not lay before me like the sun
in brilliance to shine your heart's warmth over me
and guide me through the darkest of hours.

– Just For Me –

And I am mortally wounded already, my dearest love,
knowing these guns and sabers I proudly garnish
in the fight for more sacred nights spent with you
cannot protect you from the sorrow marching your way.

I can only tell you that I cherish you beyond ends
that we define with markers of dates and names
and into the eternal I will carry your kiss upon these lips;
your touch in the deepest wounds of my soul.

Surely, love will come again to seed deep in your eyes
that a garden of happier times may grow to fill
the sparse plain of dusty reminders I will till in time
across the landscape of your memories of me.

Yet, forget me not when you tender out old music
on the piano where we sat in the courtship of youth
when tomorrow was the promise of more laughter
and the love songs were played just for me.

Where Ever You Are...

You wouldn't let me
know you
like I knew your name
without conscious effort
across my lips
imprinted on my mind
like my first understanding
of self and
all the implications
alone means

Bewitched I swirl
in memories and fantasies
and dreams where you move
in slow motion
always in slow motion . . .
gazing transfixed upon
somewhere
far beyond my reach
yet

– Where Ever You Are . . . –

Somehow I can hear
the melody of angels
in your words
I can once again
feel your body
pressed against my body
your arms locking
me in place
your hands dissolving
into my flesh
your breath sweet
upon my face

Oh, how emptiness creeps
about me like a shadow
how loneliness wears me
like a scar
how your name sings to me
a love song
Genevieve

Where ever you are . . .

The Man In The Moon

We once played seesaw on playgrounds
where strands of soft hair kissed the grass
and we ran until we were the wind
that wrinkled the forehead of that old lake.

We once climbed trees until our arms grew
leaves that drifted through summer
all the way to the fall mounds of names
written on paper bag book covers and we
counted railroad ties by twos until dark
and back home again.

We asked each other questions
without the mark or the patience
to await the answer so we made up
our own and mailed them to the stars
on the wings of wounded doves.

We stood face to face and knew
each other in the silence of our thoughts
but somewhere in the empty bottles I have
strewn across the world you climbed inside
to become a message adrift on the dead sea,
I guess in hopes to find what was once me.

Should you ever find him . . . send me the answer.
I'll be waiting in the moon.

Memories In The Dark

There is a hush that tiptoes into us
just before the fall of sheets, clothes and light
in the deep breaths of anticipation
that follows the laughter and the silence.

The moments when hummingbirds take shadow
to a speed so fast they seem not to move
just hover on the walls like picture stills
waiting to be framed in petals of gold.

Time pauses to reflect in the mirror
just long enough to remember passing
then steps itself backwards through a locked door
to peek in on memories made in the dark.

Say Not The Words

Say not the words that gather
in your precious mouth like
stars at dusk to twinkle
in the night of my life's
memory.

Let them hover on the dim
glow of this sunset
ever there to tempt my dreams
with thoughts never spoken
and not my nightmares
with regret for having
let myself go.

Tell me with your eyes
in the rains of seasons passing
and tell me with your touch
in Spring's hand upon my face.

DREAMS

The Laugh Of True Lovers

There you were again last night
framed in the mist of a dream
like the moon's reflection at midnight
in the ripples of a running stream.

I saw you through the eyes of another
as I watched him watching you
and you laughed the laugh of true lovers
like only first lovers can do.

Melting into a shadowed embrace
two hands silhouette the figure inside
like the white gloves of a silent mime
hiding behind a darkened divide.

There you were again last night
framed in the mist of a dream
like the moon's reflection at midnight
in the ripples of a running stream.

You looked out from within the vignette
into the scene of my sleep
and you smiled the smile of regret
like lost lovers when they weep.

You watched me through the eyes of another
as she watched me watching you
and you laughed the laugh of true lovers
like only lost lovers can do.

TRAVELS OF THE SAME TIME

sometimes dreams come true
and stories written are the truth
but just as dreams come true
so do nightmares too
dreams and nightmares are siblings
born of the same mind
carrying in their ragged suitcases
travels of the same time

some call the voices muses
as if they were of themselves
less a part of the writer
than the pen wrapped in hand

perhaps we are dipped
by a special ladle
from the well of souls
made up of more than ourselves
than we even know

I have known the dream
to become the truth and I
have known the nightmare
to become the dream

the souls remember
and I write

ACROSS THE DISTANCE

when the hot watered springs
of the painted desert
wash your feet
in the need to dance
know . . .
upon the grey cast shadows
of an eastern shore
cold waters soak mine
in longings to waltz

so let us transpose the dream
to the misty slopes
of majestic moors
where warm waters rise
from the mix
as feet shuffle in swirling joy

let us dance into the clouds
and down the rolling slopes
into the fertile valley
where creatures of calling
perch in mesmerized wonder
watching in jealousy

let us laugh ourselves
to the ground in dizziness
and kiss
until the dream's shades lower
and we make love
in the darkness, alone
across the distance

To Rest Upon A Calmer Shore

I know not from where this sadness comes
only that it tangles itself within my flesh
as if it were some mark of birth left to sit
upon me and spy into the cracks between
my shadow and the darkest of nights.

Even the miracle of your smile cannot tide
the jagged cliffs that tower over me
when the hurricane swirls around its own eye.

Muted rains cast fog from the tempered waves
as they toy and toss me in sheets of woe
until sickness takes me into the blue hollows
where wet hands slide apart and sink
beneath the desperate hunger of the sea.

But even the most tattered of ships return
in aftermath, to rest upon a calmer shore.
And it is there you will find the strongest of me
waiting for you to build castles in the sand.

Where A Princess Meets The Sea

The ocean is an angry dog
just beyond the breakwater
where sun scorched sailors hang
their hearts tethered to the wind in sail.

And stories reach through the mind of night
to touch unseen things less restless
than the tossing churn of broken hearts
beneath a sleepless ship.

On the midnight watch I often huddle
with tangled thoughts of the Princess by the sea
and the deck lamp's flicker listens to the poems
she sings for a Captain far greater than me.

Sometimes the seagulls are the voices
of old bones that rest under wave and wind
calling to the green fields beneath the Quantlock Hills
where rock shoaled shores line the Bridgewater Bay.

It is there in the haze of day's ending
when sleep meets the eyes of old dreams
that sailors fore and aft have seen her
tossing flowers into the heart of the sea.

'Twas a rose meant for her lover
whose thorns bled a salt dried hand
six thousand miles west of a promise
six thousand miles deep in a man.

Now my imagination carries her with me
that I may sing her words to the storms
that bind the palm of an old sailor's ghost
where a Princess meets the sea.

Dreaming Of You

There you are
In lava's glow against a moonless midnight.
Temptation beyond denial,
Smiling the distant smile of desire,
Somewhere beyond all hope.
Embedded in the dreams of faceless names
Across the web of souls.

It is strange to watch myself
Wander within the mist,
Always a reach away.
Another step to take.
Gliding above the ground
Unable to walk or run,
Just drifting towards outstretched arms
That fill an empty place.

Each dream brings no new discovery
Nor unveiling of unseen things.
No tale of distant lovers
Finding one another across the transversal of loneliness.
No thank yous said, nor good-byes.

There is no land of promise
Nor promised lands here.
Just borrowed glimpses of perfection
Returned to their rightful owner
At the end of each dream.

Twilight

Twilight opens over me
in the bloom of distant flowers
that sparkle through the violets
beyond the reach of time.
And in the haze of daylight passing
over the edge of quiet nights
the evening breeze, her fingers,
rustle the leaves of fall.

A precious fleeting touch
holds me in the arms of contentment
until the last black sand of night
drops through the hourglass passage
into the emptiness of waiting
for twilight to come again.

Forbidden Dreams

The night's eye looks down upon us
casting naked shadows that wrestle
with tangled sheets and empty shoes
left behind on the edge of lover's leap.

Our fall broken by the silence of tears
that cradle doubt in the aftermath of names
cast from quivering lips thirsty to taste
the bittersweet sanctity of surrender.

High above the cold night streets we listen
to each other's hearts healing and aching
knowing the pain is the price of having leapt
into the reality of a forbidden dream.

CURTAINS

I hung these curtains
to shield eyes
from seeing through
the window into my soul;
to hide the secrets
I fear to tell;
to decorate the humble
surroundings
within my heart.

I hung these curtains
to shield my eyes
from looking out
into the perspective
of promise;
to keep my secrets
dark;
to dim the humility
of fear.

But the curtains are not
sewn together;
not tied closed with knots;
nor hung without rings.

They are just waiting
to be opened.

There Is A Dark Spot In The Twilight

Fireflies fill the meadow
as though the deep night sky
had poured itself down across the land
to dance with the songs of a night lark
and the distant, sleepless loon.

The dew weeps from every blade of grass
that drifts into the reach of sorrow's light
falling from half the face of the moon.

Even the beetle scarred magnolia tree
seems a little closer to the sadness of moss
on this thick and muggy eve.

Voices from far across the meadow
tethered to the tepid Georgia breeze
glide by like passing strangers.

And I grasp a word from the air
tie it to another and then another
until I try to make sense of nothing.

– There Is A Dark Spot In The Twilight –

I guess somewhere high in this tree
hang the echoes of our old laughter
and the dreams we dared to tell here.

Maybe they are the leaves that sprout
each year from the memories of the wood
to remind me of the cycle of life and death.

My life, your death and the shadow of time
that forever sits underneath these branches
always here waiting for a visit from me.

And there is a dark spot in the twilight
where a bright twinkle used to be
peering down through the leaves
at two boys in this tree.

I guess, dear friend, that twinkle was in your eyes.

IN THE SKIES OF HEAVEN
A NOBLE EAGLE SOARS

In the skies of Heaven a noble Eagle soars
high above the rainbow of souls
and over the bridge to God's country's shores
across the rivers, the valleys and knolls
where the red hearts of humanity cry one tear
for the loss of the young and the old

Singed by the fires of the Devil's arrows
her talons bleed the names of the dead
and her cry echoes beyond the land of Pharaohs
across the ocean, the deserts and dreads
where the black hearts of humanity rise to cheer
for the loss of the single and the wed

Bidding in mournful sorrow
the mighty chorus sings
and the Eagle will rule tomorrow
from the Land where freedom rings

In the skies of Heaven a noble Eagle soars
high above the rainbow of souls
Singed by the fires of the Devil's arrows
her talons bleed the names of the dead
Bidding in mournful sorrow
the mighty chorus sings
and the Eagle will rule tomorrow
from the Land where freedom rings

Another Moment

I am sorry that I happened to recall
you from old days long put to rest
but this morning lifted her eyes open
to look over long paths once dusty
from the shuffle of young steps
too much in a hurry to walk slowly
with dreams.

Now the dreams call
from a distant place I left behind
somewhere on that labyrinth of turns
scratched on the doorknob
of eternity's entrance.

The promise to not look back
and remember is one I could not keep
though I have tried with all my strength.
But, that strength wanes with the gathering
of nights in the chest of sleep.

Curse me for reaching into the shadowbox
where you and I live forever at seventeen.
The plunder was not a deed meant to steal time.
No, my love. I only sought to place there
another moment to remember.

Beyond The Sound Of Waves

A single set of fading footprints
betray these notions of truth
and the soft brush of your hair
against this haggard face
in that moment's return
dissolves into the sleep
of the sun.

Still . . . I wait these
sinking feet understanding legs
that shiver in their place
unwilling to retrace lonely steps
reclaimed by the rising tide.

And I wait and I listen
far across the tattered moon
that splinters upon the sea
against a horizon of nothingness
where black, sailed ships make way.

I watch through the salty mist
that tear these hollowed eyes
in hopes to glimpse your spirit
riding on the clouds
of the night.

I listen just perchance to hear
your voice beyond the sound of waves.

Sweet Dreams

When sleep pulls you through
the adit hidden in the darkness
silently beckoning you into illusions
brewed in the broth of wishes

drink not from the chalice of nightmares
filled with bitter memories
but rather from the goblet of dreams
filled with the nectar of possibility . . .

and should I perchance
join you there upon the green
let us displace lost time
with the laughter of kindred spirits

let us hopelessly entangle ourselves
like discarded chains of jewelry
never to be untangled again
nor stored in the darkness alone

The Gentle Days Of Autumn

The gentle days of autumn
come with a soft kiss of serenity
that keeps lovers under their covers
in the brisk morning breeze.

The rustle of leaves is a concert
of nature's music played by the wind
and time walks as slow as a mime
on her path across the horizons.

All I want to do on these days
is to be as close to you as I can.
No further apart than the beat of hearts
through arms tied by clasped hands.

I want the wisps of supple hair
at the base of your neck to tickle
my nose until a smile curls our toes
in laughter spread across the meadow.

I want to carry you like a chariot
through the forest of amber and red
until every wild bird of prey flies away
to leave us in the woods all alone.

I want to imprint our shadows in clover
that even the deer shall know our names
in the flavor of green beneath a white scene
when winter paints the rainbow pale.

The gentle days of autumn
come with a soft kiss of serenity
and joy fills me with the thrills of a boy
that love may know the fall once again.

REALITIES

Again

There are moments that defy human shackles,
leaving us in their passing to remember until
perchance we should live to see them again.
Having known their glory seems less reward
than a teasing taste of too much Heaven on Earth.

Perhaps this moment is like a blood, red sunset
meant to leave me with a yearning never fulfilled.
Perhaps there is love too perfect to be painted
and happiness beyond any words to speak.

And if I walked through this unlocked door
would my shadow stay here on the outside
or would it hide in the dark place in my heart
waiting to spill out all over the floor
when the sun of our days falls to evening?

Better that I walk away and take my shadow
that it may follow me in search of this moment
while it fills the dark place in my heart until
perchance I should live to see you again.

IF I WERE

If I were a minion
   of the Marquis de Sade
I would pain myself
   just to bleed . . .
that I might touch you,
   in red.

If I were a thief
   of the darkest nights
I would steal insanity
   just to hide . . .
that I might touch you,
   in black.

If I were a ghost
   of the other side
I would scare time
   just to hover . . .
that I might touch you,
   in white.

IF LOVE WERE

If love were a fortune to pile high
in mounds of glimmer and shimmer
and shine, would I not be richer
than all the Spanish galleons ever
swallowed by the sea?

If love were a red morning wind
as lovely as the scarlet rose
with petals more soft than flame,
would I not be the voice of leaves
that rush to greet you in the fall?

If love were music with no words
just echoes that travel through bone
to gather from the first to the last
beat of this heart, would I not be
the story in all of your songs?

If love were the blue ink of a poet
spilled into a puddle beside old paper
more wanting than a handless clock
whose tick tells no time, would I not be
all the words never written?

If love were but one death,
would I not be anything
at all?

In Passing

Shadow and light are eternal lovers.
So is the way of night and day . . . in passing.
And time is a song played by the hands
of distance on black and white keys
tethered to dreams.

Mirrors hold an opposite world inside
the turning pages of this life's rewrite
and the reflection is the same, only older.

Were we only children once again and again
to reverse the play of games and begin
with rules more favorable to win.
But you can only tie fallen apples back on the limb,
you can't have them grow again and again.

The flute makes love to the wind and time . . . in passing
and my soul blisters in the flames of candles
burning away the darkness and the tune.

Turn with me, around and around,
until the walls blur into black space.
Turn with me, around and around,
until the mirror loses its face . . . in passing.

IN A PADDED ROOM

Shadows of voices
climb the walls in
a kaleidoscope of freaks
circling the square
and peeking out
from under this bed
waiting to grab
my soul's ankles;
drag me to death
behind black horses
racing
to hell in a hand-basket
locked shut with a buckle
that has no tongue.
I'll squirm like a worm
NO . . . a white maggot
to become a fly
and buzz away
through the mesh wire
and go eat some shit
out there . . .
Hey . . . HEY . . . HEYYYY
crypt keeper

– In A Padded Room –

wake up the dead man
I need a heart beat
to rush blood from my head
to my feet, my feet, my toes.
Where did my toes go?
I must have left them
in my shoes.
How can a door be a door
if it has no way out?
Perhaps I am out
and they are shut in
my secret box . . .

shhhh don't tell 'em
there is only enough room
in here for me and my toes.

THE GIVER AND THE TAKER COME TO SEE THE CLOWN'S ROSE FALL

Seated in the crowd of faces
to mingle with fear and fame,
the giver and the taker wait
for the clown without a name.

Three thousand simple hopeless souls
come to see the fat man fall
to a gasping funny death
that matters nothing . . .
nothing at all.

Just a stunt, an act it is,
a prelude they do not know
to the end of a borrowed life
at the beginning of the show.

For the giver gave the clown his paint
and a smile to wear in white and red
over the hush of loneliness
and the laughter of the dead.

But bargains come with a waiting price
guaranteed to appear on the bill
when the taker comes to claim the tax
for deep waters that always run still.

The blinding cone of inverted light
marks the circle of mankind's shame
around the empty silhouette
of the clown with no name.

– The Giver And The Taker Come To See The Clown's Rose Fall –

Three thousand faces turn to eyes
that stare at the thornless rose
held in the hand of a fat, funny man
with a stop light for a nose.

They point and sway and cast away
what truths they wish not to know
about themselves on mirrored shelves
behind the scenes of the show.

A single rose and a stop light nose
two shoes as big as a boat.
A painted smile on a life long frown
above words stuck in his throat.

The taker cometh in the light
and down falls the thornless rose
to the laughter of three thousand souls
never heard by the clown
with the stop sign nose.

I Saw You In A Photo

The image stops time in mid breath
an inhale or exhale, I know not
holding my breath, with you.
There is no name here, no date,
no address, no place to look
except everywhere . . .

Carousel

painted wild
wooden horses
eyes telling
instants of fear
transposed
to tiny riders
held in
the saddle
of musical terror
by dizzy dads
laughing

THE SPIDER AND THE WASP

She, patient enough to weave
a tapestry of death from silk.
He, too impatient to notice.

She, covered by darkness, hidden.
He, too vain to be discreet.

She, eyes shining, tempt the curious.
He, curious, eyes shining.

She, grey and black, fangs
wet with anticipation.
He, red tailed and bold
enough to die.

She waits, just out of reach
of the barbed stinger that
would violate her.
He, beats his wings violently,
flying nowhere but in circles
around his own tail.

She, tip-toes across the trap
wraps him in his own struggle.
He, struggles to exhaustion,
concedes the fight and sleeps
forever hers.

A Fan Walked Its Wind

a fan walked its wind
across our tangled bodies
in the heat of a hot summer
morning wrapped in white
sheets printed with U.S. in blue
letters sent across the ocean
to soldiers destined to die
in one way or another

two brown bodies burnt by love
on the beaches of a jungle oven
where death and truth hid in bushes
always stalking momentary calm

bravery diminished to the ordinary
acts of a play without curtains
where tragedy became a theme
unmentioned in our lines

nights spent drinking poison water
mixed in the dark pool of your eyes
that closed in each of our long kisses
like a padded door to sanity

– A Fan Walked Its Wind –

sweat as salty as the old fisherman
dripped from your body to mine
the harbor of my days with flowers
as red and yellow as a coward

a fan walked its wind
across our tangled bodies
in the heat of a hot summer
morning wrapped in white
sheets printed with U.S. in blue
letters sent across the ocean
to soldiers destined to die
in one way or another

Concerto Of The Pen In Ink Minor

These stains will have no wand to guide them
nor strings to rise in octaves to harmonize
with the melody of flutes and bassoons that
make love to the piano rifts adrift in key of me.

I know only the verse of words to sing
in notes that fold to hide in jewelry boxes
where plastic swans swim in black lakes
that mirror cold stones cut of sad songs.

Sheets of music tangle themselves in feet
of meter and rhythm and beat and rhyme
to parley unity into structure that flows
across the damned like a violin's bow.

But only I hear the lark of bells ring
from the old stage of sole survivors
who count crushed red velvet seats
on an empty bus to the end of time.

And I dance with paper hand shadows
on the swoon of the arm of the moon
while writing my songs out of tune
in the doorless key of this ink minor.

WITHOUT MERCY

the wrinkled and bony hands
of sorrow wail upon me without mercy
until blood, tears, mucus and drool
gather in ink blots on my nakedness
where they dry into tattoos
pressed into my flesh by the fingernails
of your minions while they dig for my heart

there to yank it from my chest
and giggle as it beats in their hands
while others dance in the cavity
its absence leaves for you

and I know there they shall mock me
in your voices and kiss me
with open mouths that taste of hate
but they shall not let me bleed enough
to die, only enough to gaze in shock
as you gnaw upon the bones

Beyond The Length Of This Reach

Deep within the violet glow
of eyes burning blue . . . I could be.
Yet, no leaps I dare take
upwards to the lambent view.
No rise I dare make
to the gates of your heart.
For these steps are merely
guides down from the chance
that they might have opened
for me.
The painted canvas
of your passions
that I so long to emblazon
with the firelight
of eternal devotion
hover high above
the length of this reach.
Yet, I surely see the unveiled
glory of every vine and flower
that I might touch and smell
and taste along the glorious
rise into the clouds
adrift upon each beckon
of your longings . . .

– Beyond The Length Of This Reach –

Oh, but I know the truth.
The iron truth that bars
me on the outside
of your knowing
while leaving me looking up
deep into the violet
of eyes burning blue.
No, it is not I who am
the rider upon your cirrus horse.
It is I who shall seat the wind
that you shall never see.

Once Spoken

The words once seeped
from my heart
like the fertile kisses
of seasons impassioned
and now they slumber
underneath the shadow
of a concave tongue
curled to speak
yet voiceless . . .
the minions of self doubt
striking them down
to mortality
where they
hide in shame
for having thought
perhaps they were
worth saying at all.
The need to be loved is a want
left beyond spoken words
deep in the memory
of silent thoughts . . .
thoughts of seasons long passed
and words never said.

TO THESE ENDS

to these ends I am scattered
like the newly fallen snow
reaching beyond the horizon
of your footsteps over the curve
of tomorrow into the wasteland
of memories . . .

memories embedded into
the emptiness of bottles
once filled with messages that
I swallowed in shallow breaths
until the darkness hid your face
behind the pain
of forgetting . . .

forgetting the bending agony
of love's hunger to be fed

UNITY OF LONELINESS

We find ourselves
huddled alone
in solitude together
across the unity
of loneliness.

We come from the same
different places
with the same
different faces
that laugh the pain
to life from death
in smiling frowns
that breathe no breath.

We touch the invisible
places we have been
in timeless travels
across nowhere
and yet we find
nothing
in the something
of our search
except the one
thing
we cannot lose . . .
ourselves.

– Unity Of Loneliness –

Each little death
giving birth to life
we shamelessly
shy away from truth
in the falsehood
of reality
that gathers clouds
on the ground.

Forever locked
in a moment
free of restraint
while tied
to the fate
of chance.

THE LAST LOVE LETTER I'LL EVER WRITE (TO YOU)

It takes such little effort to remember
And all the strength I can summon
To turn away from these memories.
In all the traveled years of distance
I have placed between those nights and these,
I am no further away from you than I was then.
Even now, I can close these aging eyes
And see every moment I spent with you
In vivid reels of Technicolor euphoria.
So vivid every taste, every smell, every sound
Rushes forward like the unleashed waters
Of a swollen river breaking through
A pitifully inadequate dam.
A dam made of the inability to forget.
If I could, I would cease to remember.
You would disappear as fast as the instant of time
That just dissolved into these thoughts.
If only that were possible in any other way
Than to die as a side effect.
No, I will keep them and wear them like the pain
Of age and fight against them on rainy days and
Lonely, cold, winter nights when I write.
I will sleep, dreamless sleep.
You can hide in the suburban darkness
Of a distant town behind the shadow of someone
Who took my place and be loved by sons
Without the name I had so longed for them to have.
You can dream in restful sleep for I will not venture
To find you. I will not tell you
That I love you nor speak of you again.
Except, perhaps, with my last breath.

Forever Searching

Your absence left me
forever searching, in every place
to find the part of me
                        displaced
beyond the edges of contentment
where agony masquerades as memory.

Each moment of laughter became
a precarious walk along the ledge
until a lack of balance
sent me

        f
         a
          l
           l
            i
              n
                g

Forever searching,
for a place
to land.

IN THE FLIRT CHATROOM

They parry
with electronic swords
too dull to cut,
protected in anonymity
behind masks
that veil truth.
They tease
with sexual feathers
plucked from birds
that fly in fantasies
left prisoner
in their dreams,
while laughing
in three letter codes
of unspoken speech.
They paint
illusions over reflections
of themselves
in VGA mirrors
and cast them like spells,
bewitching each other
into believing
they have been befriended
by the gods.

– In The Flirt Chatroom –

They return
again and again
to be whipped
by fonted straps,
knowing others cannot scar
the skin of an apparition.
They hide
in open space,
invisible to everyone
but themselves.

When

the tongue of the bell
grew too long to ring
the melody of union
and wedding white faded
to yesterday yellow
in boxes marked "when"

I was more than myself
in you

trample the paths to glory
let me hover on the first
ring of purgatory to wander
in the mist of regret
and forever listen to agony
drift across the holy sea

for that day I died
in the silence of the bell

fall upon the stage
here in my heart and cry
until the memory of my eyes
drift into the names of children

let me be less than myself
without you
for that day I died
in the silence of the bell

I Thought

I thought forever was past
the age of regret
further over the mountains
than the edge of the sea
deeper into forgiveness
than the roots of an ancient tree.

I thought forever was longer
than the arms of Satan
further over the fires of Hell
than the pit of lost souls
deeper into understanding
than an embedded splinter.

I thought forever was more distant
than inward contemplation
further over the shoulder of death
than its shadow cast
deeper into your headstone
than weathered dates.

Golden Words

There I am in your hand
high above your head
listening for the golden words
you never said.

There I am on your knee
bouncing up and down
looking for the golden words
you never found.

There I am at your side
standing all alone
wondering if the golden words
are said in your other home.

There I am in tasseled blue
a little boy no more
craving for the golden words
you never said before.

There I am in jungle green
pale and scared to death
hoping for the golden words
to float upon your breath.

– Golden Words –

There I am with a child
that you did not deserve
telling her the golden words
that I never heard.

There I am at your bed
watching you breathe to death
waiting for the golden words
to float upon your breath.

There I am at your side
standing all alone
wondering if the golden words
are said in your other home.

ON THE DEATH OF HER FATHER

Our hands grasped for each other
a last good-bye, and I drifted to
the shadows just beyond light
that dimmed quickly near
the window where a winter
scene outside mingled
with a winter scene inside
on white sheets and silver rails
in front and behind me in time.

And the snow fell around them
and through them, down into the
depths of the night.

She lay there next to him
her head upon his chest.
His hand upon her head.
Words drifting slowly
from his chilled lips
like snowflakes
from the sky . . .

– On The Death Of Her Father –

"The time is near my child
and soon I will be gone, but
lay here with me and remember
the days we shared life's song.
Know that I have loved you
from before your birth, and
I love you in this death, for upon
your hair will rest my last breath
and upon your face the memory
of the last place my heart ever beat
for you."

And the snow fell around them
and through them, down into
the depths of the night.

The Last Parade

He walked slowly
with an open gate
on crippled shoes
older than the street.
Head lowered
ducking the cheers,
waved flags
fluttering,
in unison with
the songs of warriors.
Timid gazes
flashing from
drooping eyes
underneath a hat
adorned with clasps
of silver and gold.
When's and where's
tacked to
cloth like memos
of remembrance.
Thank yous accepted
from strangers
he will never know.
Youth fading into
the distant haze
of a soldier's march
beyond
his last parade.

Museum Of The Dead

Adorned with fluttering symbols
Of beguiled freedoms
Each elongated plus
Of white stone
Rising above the tranquil green
Adds to the solemn total
Of sons and fathers
Sent to a distant place
Beyond the hopes of humans
Where sacrifice is a lament
To the Angels of peace
Aligned in rows and columns
To perpetuate some order
From the magnitude of malady
That dissected their bodies
They are housed here for eternity
In morbid remembrance
Of humanity's triumphant failures

In The Breath Of Music

The aroma of music
drifts across the vague landscape
from deep within the silhouettes
of moon-cast shadows,
effortlessly gliding across the silence,
to caress the face of sorrow
with a tender hand.
Too briefly it lingers
beneath a sigh of restitution and
chills of remembrance
reverberate in the aftershock
of return from distant places
long ago displaced.
As the melody of her touch
fades like the end of youth
I melt into timelessness,
where these illusions
reveal their untold secrets
to the eyes of eternity.
There to be unveiled

as the truth
in the breath of music
with each replay
of the tune.

Without Term

sliding down
ecliptic transversals
through paths crossing
in dimensions
of borrowed time
where salient images
emerge from darkness
as cropped stills
out of focus
on waving sheets
of opaque cloth
disappearing as quickly
as they arrived
leaving behind
debts to eternity
that can never be
paid in full
only appeased
in installments
of compounded interest
without term

Solus

distant howls
of mournful wails
drift through frosted pane

dusty mist
shaken loose
from empty old frames

neon lights
dried blood red
paint the winter rain

starless skies
bleeding black
filled with lonely pain

wrinkled rest
in flowered sheets
laugh with mute disdain

open diary
too few words
I shan't be hurt again

razor sharp
the tool of death
relief without restraint

devil's time
dripping torture
down a hollow drain

Shackled

Do not try to understand me.
It would be a futile guess to
the riddle I have become.
For I do not know, myself,
nor would I recognize such
a vision
even if it appeared as a reflection
in the mirrors of my eyes.
I would just shrug it off
as another apparition
come to haunt me again.

Do not toil or ponder
searching for a key of salvation
to unlock me from within myself.
I am shackled in lockless irons,
held by a short chain of sanity
binding me to the walls of madness.

Just love me
from an arms length
so that I may keep the chains taut
and maybe, one day,
break them
when I reach for you.

Listen To The Violins

It is time for me to go
beyond the reality of death
into the melody of songs
played on the strings of violins.

And as time caresses your heart
easing the pain of being left behind
close your eyes my love and listen
to my voice in each draw of the bow.

Let me drift to you and through you
then gather in swirls around you
that make the candle flame dance
and the shadows will be me reaching.

And when you cry yourself to sleep
I'll be waiting in the wisps of your dreams
flying on the notes of old love songs
played on the strings of violins.

UNENDED

Trampled heart
ripped apart
left to bleed
unmended.

Shattered dream
sweating scream
left to cry
untended.

Open book
a page took
the story left
unended.

IN THE PASSING OF BREATHS

I know in the passing of breaths
all that once lived of you in me
will become the sharp, thin edges
of shades that close when I sleep.

Sleep that shall become deaths
painted on a black velvet canopy
waving above untrimmed hedges
surrounding the garden weeds I keep.

Weeds weaved into ragged wreaths
hanging over the you left in me
on a nail pounded in the wedges
between tears and the need to weep.

Wheels On A Cloud

There is a place only I can go
where faces crumble like falling rock
over the edges of my mind
into the blank abyss of madness.
But even in the darkness there is
laughter.

"and they shall laugh as they gather,
to shackle him in black thorns and he
shall cry in pain"

How funny can it be to kill a man
when he is already dead?
Not in the death of mortality
but as dead as the waterless sea
and as useless as wheels on a
cloud.

"and they shall ascend upon the angel,
to cut out his heart of gold and blood
shall fall in the heavens"

I guess my whole life I've picked flowers

for my own grave.

Tony Spivey

TONY SPIVEY

Tony Spivey was born in Soperton, Georgia, and graduated from Vidalia High School in Vidalia, Georgia. After 16 years of active duty service in the United States Marine Corps, Tony's military career was cut short due to a service related disability.

While undergoing rehabilitation he attended and graduated from East Carolina University with a B.S. in Middle Grades Education with concentrations in Language Arts and Mathematics. He also earned an advanced certification as a K-12 Reading Specialist.

It was in college that Tony began to write. In 1996, his play *A Civil Outpost* was produced. In 1997, his poem *I'm Leaving*, won first place in poetry during the East Carolina University Literary and Arts competition. In 2000, his poem *Ceramic Clown*, won first prize in the Webstatic.com semi-annual poetry competition.

Since that time his poetry has gained him critical acclaim across the world through the Internet and led to the publication of *Covered Ground*. Tony currently lives and teaches in New Bern, North Carolina.

INDEX

3 A.M. At The Veterans Hospital ©1997 page 56
A Cry Of Understanding ©2001 page 26
A Fan Walked Its Wind ©2002 page 136
A Poet Should Not Die Unwritten ©2002 page 4
Acknowledgments page xiii
Across The Distance ©2000 page 112
Again ©2002 page 126
All I Ever Wanted To Do ©1999 page 22
Another Moment ©2002 page 121
As If ©1999 page 52
Ashes ©2002 page 101
Beyond The Fall ©2002 page 95
Beyond The Length Of This Reach ©2001 page 140
Beyond The Sound Of Waves ©2001 page 122
Black Rain ©2000 page 69
Black Sleep ©2002 page 94
Blame Me ©2001 page 84
Blue Pennies Down ©2002 page 87
Brush Strokes ©2001 page 80
Captured ©2002 page 92
Carousel ©2001 page 134
Ceramic Clown ©2000 page 7
Concerto Of the Pen In Ink Minor ©2001 page 138
Covered Ground ©2002 page 36
Curtains ©1996 page 117
Dance Of The Hummingbirds In June ©2002 page 28
Dead Stars ©2000 page 34
Dedication page v
Dreaming Of You ©2000 page 115
Driftwood And Seafoam ©2001 page 32
Eight Thousand Days ©2001 page 80
First Kiss ©2000 page 60
First Light Of Day ©2001 page 81

– Index –

Forbidden Dreams ©2000 page 116
Forever Searching © 2000 page 147
Forgotten ©1996 page 5
Gently ©2002 page 90
Golden Words ©1999 page 152
Holding On ©2001 page 78
How Could It Be? ©2001 page 27
I Ache ©1999 page 55
I Am The Sea ©2002 page 84
I Don't Know ©1999 page 18
I Know Her In Words ©2001 page 76
I Love You ©2000 page 47
I Saw You In A Photo ©1999 page 134
I Thought ©2000 page 151
If I Were ©2002 page 127
If Love Were ©2002 page 128
I'm Leaving ©1997 page 44
In A Padded Room ©2002 page 130
In Passing ©2002 page 129
In The Breath of Music ©2000 page 158
In The Flirt Chatroom ©1998 page 148
In The Passing of Breaths ©2001 page 164
In The Rain ©2000 page 54
In The Skies of Heaven
   A Noble Eagle Soars ©2001 page 120
Just For Me ©2002 page 102
Just For You ©1999 page 54
Listen To The Violins ©2000 page 162
Love Verse ©2000 page 40
Memories In The Dark ©2002 page 107
Mr. Adelson Speaks To My
   Love In The Park ©2002 page 30
Museum Of The Dead ©2001 page 157

– Index –

My Love Is A Simple Love ©2002 page 88
Oh, How I Loved You ©2000 page 20
Old Jill, Dad And Me ©1996 page 12
On A Gray, Dusty Wall ©1998 page 50
On Highway 43 ©1999 page 46
On The Death Of Her Father ©2000 page 154
Once ©2001 page 6
Once Spoken ©2001 page 142
Passing Time At The China Doll ©1998 page 48
Quantum Kisses In The
   Ethereal Garden ©2001 page 62
Quietly Wicked ©2001 page 75
Rain On The Window ©1996 page 97
Say Not The Words ©2000 page 108
Secret Love ©2000 page 68
Secrets Scripted ©2002 page 86
Shackled ©2000 page 161
Shadow Dancing ©2001 page 74
She Is ©2002 page 85
Silence In The Wood ©2000 page 32
Solus ©1999 page 160
Sometimes ©2002 page 100
Sweet Dreams ©2000 page 123
Table Of Contents page vii
Tamed ©1998 page 37
Tangled Heart Strings ©2000 page 67
That Day ©2002 page 33
The Gentle Days Of Autumn ©2002 page 124
The Giver And The Taker Come To See
   The Clown's Rose Fall ©2002 page 132
The Last Love Letter I'll Ever
   Write (To You) ©2000 page 146
The Last Parade ©2000 page 156

– Index –

The Laugh Of True Lovers ©1997 page 110
The Man In The Moon ©2001 page 106
The Moaning Well ©2000 page 42
The Peep Hole ©1999 page 59
The Procession ©1996 page 96
The Silence Of Alone ©1999 page 51
The Spider And The Wasp ©2002 page 135
The Taste Of Her Soul ©2002 page 91
The Vessel Of Innocence ©2000 page 8
The Violets Of Our Youth ©2000 page 16
There Is A Dark Spot
   In The Twilight ©2002 page 118
This Love Is Not Misplaced ©2002 page 89
This Morning, I Just
   Watched You Sleep ©2000 page 38
To Rest Upon A Calmer Shore ©2001 page 113
To Steal From The Devil ©2002 page 82
To These Ends ©2001 page 143
Tonight ©2001 page 77
Tony Spivey Biography page 167
Too Well ©1992 page 11
Toothpaste And Underwear ©2001 page 72
Touch My Hand That I May See ©2001 page 74
Travels Of the Same Time ©2002 page 111
Twilight ©2001 page 116
Under The Glow Of The Moon ©2000 page 61
Unended ©1998 page 163
Unity Of Loneliness ©2001 page 144
Until Time Bows Me Old ©2000 page 40
Wheels On A Cloud ©2002 page 165
When ©2001 page 150
When I Sit Silently Beside You ©2001 page 70
When We Loved Each Other ©1999 page 24

– Index –

Where A Princess Meets The Sea ©2002 page 114
Where Ever You Are ©2000 page 104
Wild Horses ©2002 page 98
Windless Chimes ©2001 page 71
Without Mercy ©2001 page 139
Without Regret ©2000 page 83
Without Term ©1999 page 159
Your Embrace ©2000 page 68
Your Hands ©2001 page 41

www.ingramcontent.com/pod-product-compliance
Lightning Source LLC
Chambersburg PA
CBHW071711090426
42738CB00009B/1738